This book belongs to

....

For Rafiki yangu, Helen—
AKA Twiga.
CG

For Mum and Dad,
SU

Published in 2021 by Welbeck Editions
An Imprint of Welbeck Children's Limited,
part of Welbeck Publishing Group.

20 Mortimer Street, London W1T 3JW

ISBN 978 1 91351 932 2

Printed in Dongguan, China

10 9 8 7 6 5 4 3 2 1

FSC
www.fsc.org
MIX
Paper from
responsible sources
FSC® C020056

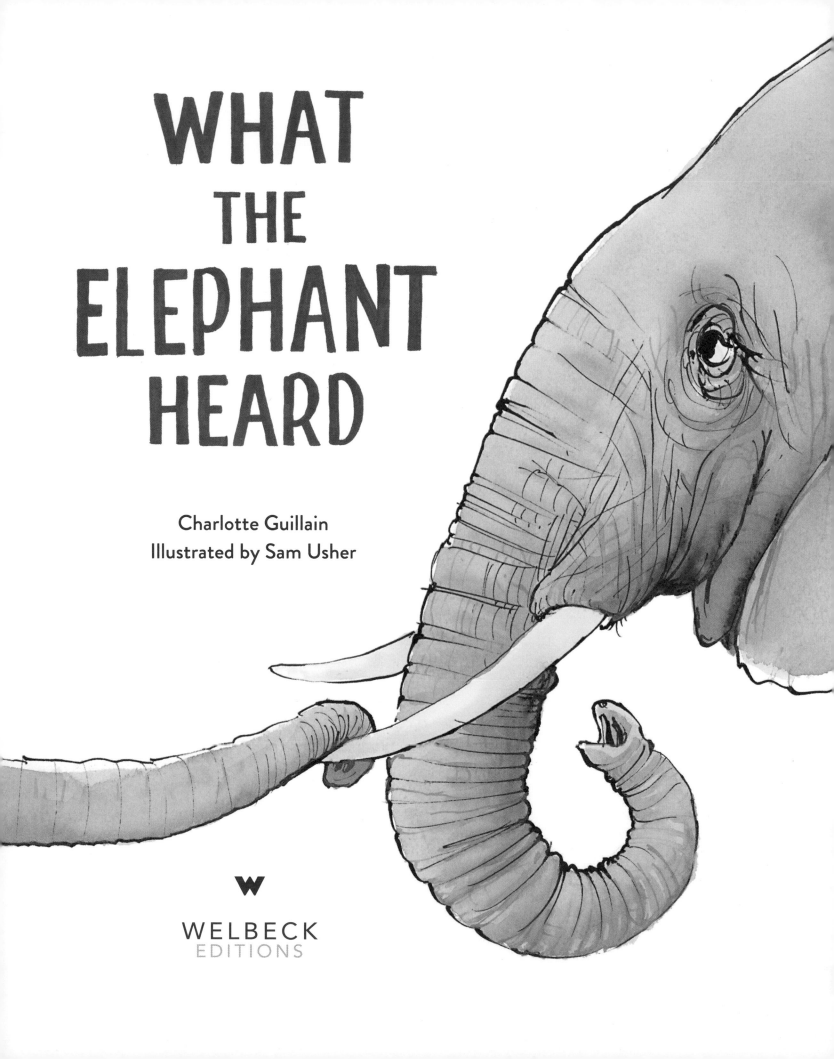

WHAT THE ELEPHANT HEARD

Charlotte Guillain
Illustrated by Sam Usher

W

WELBECK
EDITIONS

Here on the savanna, I live with my herd.
I'll tell you our history—hear every word.
My grandmother has so much knowledge to share.
She leads us to water, she somehow knows where.

Before she was born, other grandmothers led.
Each shared all the stories she held in her head,
of huge zebra herds that came thundering by,
the roaring of lions, the bee-eater's cry.

But then came strange humans and new sounds rang out:
a clanking of metal, spades scraping, fierce shouts.
They brought their machines that pumped clouds in the sky,
and shrieked like hyenas as they clattered by.

My great-grandma knew every place on these plains.
She knew when the wildebeests followed the rains.
And in the dry season, she knew where to go
to find ancient places where water would flow.

When Grandma was born and was just a small calf,
the grasslands still thronged with gazelles and giraffe.
She heard the low growl of the planes in the sky,
the rattle of cars as the tourists drove by.

As Grandma grew older, new sounds filled the plain:
the grind of great trucks, like a groaning of pain.
Then saws buzzed and whined as the trees were cut down
and carried away to the people in town.

When I was a calf, fences lay in our way—
we heard angry shouts and were driven away.
The bellowing cattle were all we could hear.
We couldn't reach water, although it was near.

Then one day we froze at a trumpeting sound—
a gunshot rang out and then echoed around.
We waited till sunset. The poachers had fled,
away from the place where my father lay—dead.

And now we are waiting for thunder and rain.
We wait for the wildebeest rumble again.
The land is dust-dry and the sun bakes the ground.
Can Grandma still show us where water is found?

We cross the savanna, so weary and weak.
The land all around us looks empty and bleak.
But wait—what's that smell? There's a water hole near!
Now as we move on again . . .

... what will we hear?

All about Elephants

There are two species of elephant in Africa: African savanna (*Loxodonta Africana*) and African forest (*Loxodonta cyclotis*). There is also another species of elephant that lives in Asia.

There is usually one leader in a female herd, the matriarch. She is usually the oldest female and leads her daughters and their calves. The matriarch has the experience and knowledge to help the herd survive by finding water and food and avoiding danger.

A very useful trunk

An elephant's trunk is made up of its upper lip and nose. It can grow to be over 6.5 feet (2 m) long and weigh as much as 300 pounds (140 kg). An elephant can use its trunk to pick up tiny objects, comfort other elephants, defend itself, push over trees, and suck up water to drink.

A pretty cool skin

The skin of an elephant can be up to 1 inch (2.5 cm) thick. Elephants roll in mud and dust to remove bugs from their skin and keep cool. Elephants' ears are designed to pump blood around them to help cool the elephant down under the hot African sun. The more the ears flap, the hotter the elephant is.

What about the male elephants?

Male or bull elephants are also known as "bachelors." When they become adults, they leave their mothers and often join other males in small groups. They don't reach full size until they are around 35 years old, so they can spend about half their life growing!

Talking to each other

Elephants can communicate with each other using around 70 different calls. These range from deep rumbles to loud trumpets. It's thought that they can also sense seismic waves traveling through the ground using their sensitive feet.

Faster than you'd think

African elephants can walk up to 120 miles (195 km) per day, but usually only cover around 15 miles (25 km) each day. When they need to, they can run at speeds of 40 miles per hour (60 kmh).

Growing old, growing big

A male elephant can grow as tall as 13 feet (4 m) and weigh up to 7 tons. The average African elephant has a life span of about 70 years. That's a long time to remember where to find the best sources of water!

Mighty teeth

Elephants' tusks are extra-long incisor teeth that start to grow when they are about two years old. Male elephants' tusks can weigh over 220 pounds (100 kg). Elephants have six sets of teeth that grow one set after another, throughout their lives. Most have started to use their final set by the age of 50.

A big appetite

African elephants are herbivores and only eat grasses, herbs, fruit, plants, and trees. An African elephant can eat as much as four to seven per cent of its body weight every day! Elephants know how to dig down into dry river beds with their feet, trunk, and tusks to find water under the ground.

Caring for Elephants

Orphan rescue

Sometimes an elephant calf is left alone without its mother. Luckily, there are organizations that take care of orphaned baby elephants.

Rescue teams hurry to help a stranded calf as quickly as possible, giving it milk and medicine before carefully transporting it back to the orphanage. Once the baby elephant is there, it is helped by a human caregiver all the time. The calf will be very upset to have lost its mother and herd and needs a gentle, caring keeper to take care of it around the clock.

The keeper acts as if they are the calf's new mother. This involves feeding the calf milk every three hours and sleeping with it every night! As the calf recovers from its terrifying experience, the keeper helps it play and learn the skills it will need as it grows up and hopefully returns to the wild. The keeper takes the calf out for walks with other orphans every day so it can explore the environment safely and become stronger and more confident.

The calves at the orphanage become a new family herd. Older female orphans learn how to take the lead and look after the rest of the group, just as females do in the wild. From the age of about three, the orphaned calves stop drinking milk and gradually learn how to live back in the wild. Eventually they make friends with and learn from herds of wild elephants. After what can be many years, the young elephants are finally ready to leave the orphanage and join a wild herd. But they sometimes come back to visit the keepers who spent so much time taking care of them when they were babies.

One of the reasons elephant calves are orphaned is poaching. Poachers kill adult elephants for their tusks, including mothers with young calves. Fortunately, there are brave men and women who work as rangers to protect elephants from poachers.

Wildlife rangers

Wildlife rangers need many skills as well as great courage. They also need to be in excellent shape and complete extensive training before starting the job. They must know the vast terrain under their protection—and the wildlife living there—extremely well. They're also trained in the law and to help educate people living on the savanna to value and protect wild animals. They patrol a huge area, tracking elephant herds and other endangered animals and keeping a lookout for poachers.

Rangers sometimes have to live out in the field for months at a time, protecting wild animals both day and night. Their job is to scare poachers away or arrest them, which can be very dangerous.

As well as protecting elephants and rhinoceroses from poachers, rangers help animals that have been caught in snares set by hunters and help to prevent trees from being cut down illegally. It's a tough, demanding job, but the rangers are helping save elephants' lives every day.

Drone

Laptop

Binoculars

Compass

Camera

Be a Friend to the Elephants

Savanna elephants, like the herd in this book, are still found in eastern and southern Africa, but their numbers have declined dramatically. In the 1970s there were around 1.3 million elephants living in Africa. Now there are only an estimated 400,000 left. This is mainly due to their habitat being destroyed for farming and climate change causing rivers to dry up, making it harder for wildlife to find water. Humans are also killing elephants for their tusks (ivory). Elephant ivory is used to make carvings that are mostly sold in Asia, despite an international ban on this trade. Poachers in African countries can make a lot of money killing elephants and selling their tusks.

We can help elephants by supporting organizations that protect them. For example, the World Wildlife Fund works hard to help fight against poachers and avoid problems between humans and elephants who share the same land. Conservationists track and monitor elephant herds and help rangers protect them and other wild animals. We can donate to these organizations or sponsor an elephant. Tourists visiting Africa can help by bringing money into local communities, which will work hard to protect their local wildlife. We can also tell our friends and families about the problems elephants face to raise awareness and help them thrive again.

Be a Local
Wildlife Hero

You can help wildlife closer to home, too. Find out which animals where you live are endangered and tell your friends and family. If you allow wildflowers to grow in your yard you'll encourage insects, and you can also put food and water out for birds. Never leave litter on the ground when you are out and about—pick up everything you take with you and leave things as you find them. There might be local wildlife projects that you can hep with to protect living things in your environment—for example, events organized by the National Wildlife Federation (www.nwf.org) or the Audubon Society (www.audubon.org).

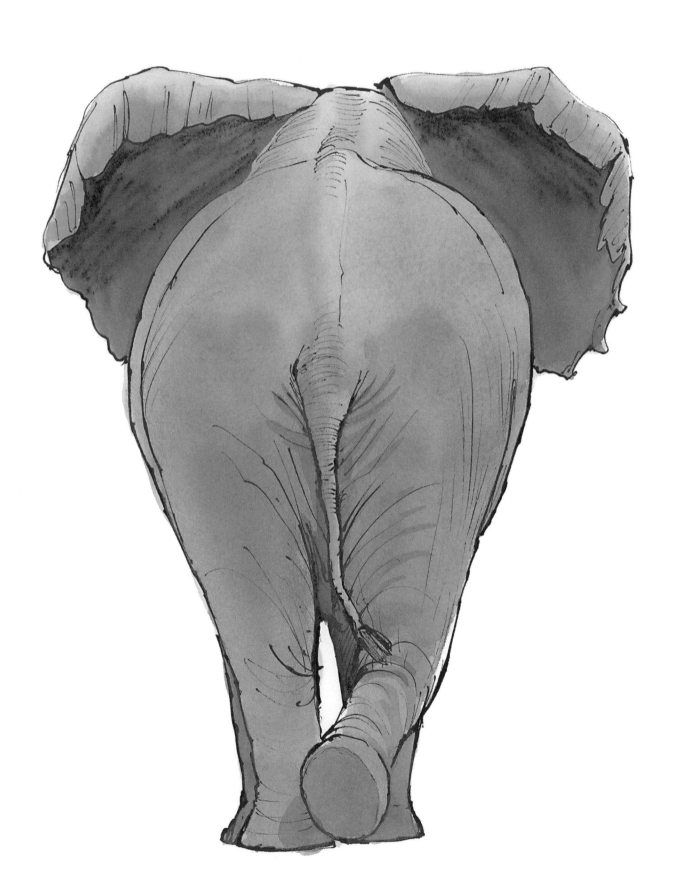